TINA COULSTING CARTER (née Risley), BA (Hons), MA, PGCHE, is the inventor of *The Presentation X-Factor* formula, which has taken the pain out of preparing presentations and helped hundreds of people to gain confidence in themselves and their ability to stand up and present their ideas.

She is the co-founder of Mentor Communications Consultancy and a renowned specialist in presentation and communication skills development. Formerly a university teacher Tina has devised an approach that builds self-assurance and enables speedy development of transferable communication and influencing skills.

Applying her expertise to management and professional learning programmes she has, since 1999, worked with many organisations and individuals on pitch presentations, conference rehearsals and personal development for leadership.

Illustrations:
Øivind Hovland & Tina Coulsting Carter

Second Edition.
Published in paperback 2012
by Mentor Press
part of Mentor Communications Consultancy Ltd.
www.mentorltd.co.uk

First published in Great Britain in 2009 by Silverwood Books
Copyright © Tina Coulsting Carter 2009

ISBN 9780957224339

Set in 11pt Trade Gothic by Mentor Press
Printed and bound in UK by Whitehall Printing

Get The Presentation X-Factor!

Everything you need to know to develop your personal
presentation and gain confidence to inspire others

by

Tina Coulsting Carter

I would like to dedicate this book to my husband, children and any one who has stood in front of an audience with their heart thumping.

Contents

Introduction

Communication is something most of us take for granted but the fact is that some of us are better at it than others – for all sorts of reasons that could be partly genetic, cultural, social or educational. Some people have lively and communicative families, others don't, and some are invested with communication skills at school – although not many in any overt way it has to be said.

Most people are never taught how to make a presentation, even at universities where many of us start the painful process of standing up in front of other people to present our ideas. We tend to learn to speak at our mother's knee and don't really think too much about how we present ourselves until we move into the world of work.

I've written this book not only for all of you who are now faced with the challenge of making presentations to colleagues, staff, conferences, meetings, but also for those who have experience of making presentations but somehow have never quite fathomed why they are sometimes successful and sometimes not.

The reason I've written it is because I firmly believe that wherever you come from and whatever your background you can learn to be an excellent presenter. With the right approach, as described in this book, anyone can become the sort of presenter who can inspire others.

I myself am not naturally extrovert and was shy and painfully inarticulate at the start of my adult years. The UK is a very literary society, and like many others I developed my writing skills at university. It wasn't until I began working as a multi-media designer at the end of the Eighties that I woke up to the fact that presentation skills are something that can be worked on and developed as well – and not only that, most of us would benefit from working on them.

The seed was sown when I was working in the early days of inter-active video and was lucky enough to be involved with a train-ing programme about making presentations – starring Mel Smith as it happens. Mel played Christopher Columbus pitching to the King and Queen of Spain for funds to discover America!

Later, while teaching students how to make television news programmes at the University of the West of England, I started analysing in earnest what makes a good presenter.

Charles Handy (one of my favourite business and leadership guru and author of books such as *Inside Organisations, New Alchemists and Re-invented lives)* says that when you teach you learn more than your students and that's certainly my experi-ence.

When I was asked to run workshops in making presentations for science students, as part of a forward thinking degree course called Science, Society and the Media, I really needed to unravel the mysteries of what makes a good presentation. At the same time I recognised that I was going to have to practice what I preached. To get the young people in front of me to change into authoritative and confident presenters of their research and reports, I myself needed to inspire them.

Life had played a clever trick on me by forcing me to change

*Your body language can be as manically
enthusiastic as you like, but you also need
a strong message to have real impact.*

and develop my communication skills so that I could help other people change and develop theirs.

That was over fifteen years ago. I currently work with managers at all levels, from chief executives to team leaders, on developing communication and presentation skills. The expertise I'd built up around teaching transferable skills got me head-hunted and in 1998 I became a co-founder of Mentor Consultancy.

My knowledge in the area of communication and presentation skills was seen as a valuable asset within the corporate and public sector organisations I started working with. It wasn't long before I understood what an essential skill presentation is to anyone wishing to gain influence in business, whether that be to win new clients or to win hearts and minds in a quest for leadership success.

Since those enjoyable days devising fun sessions for undergraduates, I've continued with my mission to help trainees develop their presentation skills in the most practical and empowering way. I eventually recognised that what was missing from a lot of the material I read on the subject was any sense of the psychology around the business of addressing audiences.

Many people learn about positive body language and that you must 'tell them what you are going to tell them, tell them and tell them again' – but what do you tell them and more to the point how do you tell them? Your body language can be as manically enthusiastic as you like but if you don't get your message right then you can't have any real impact. And vice versa – your content may be brilliant but if you deliver it in a boring way then people will not listen.

The real insight comes with knowing what you want to say and how to say it in a way that specifically targets the audience in front of you.

Using psychology to start to understand audiences and what they need is the first step to becoming an excellent presenter. Even better than that, the confidence this brings ensures that you'll enjoy making presentations and take away a sense of achievement every time you talk in front of others.

This book shows you how to get to that point. It brings together lots of things you already know, together with my own Presentation X-Factor formula for structuring presentations, in a way that will make this subject click for you once and for all. It will help you to get The Presentation X-Factor!

But first, a little reflection on where you are now with presentation and why reading this book is a really good move…

Wherever you come from,
whoever you are
you can learn to be inspiring
when speaking to others.

The only real
prerequisite is that you
must want to be –
and care about being –
a good communicator.

Chapter 1

Why You Should Do It!

If you are reading this then it means you have made a conscious decision to improve your personal presentation in some way. Maybe you've seen others who have 'the X-Factor' and decided you want it too. Perhaps you've just accepted a promotion at work and giving presentations will be expected of you where they might not have been before. Whatever the reason you've embarked along this route – you've already taken the biggest step, just by wanting to change.

Let me encourage you further because I firmly believe that by developing communication and presentation skills, you can transform your life for the better permanently.

These skills are transferable into every part of your life and will help you whether you are addressing large conferences or trying to get ideas across in one-to-one meetings, personal or work-related. During the course of this book, I'll show you how to build rapport with audiences and individuals. This will in turn strengthen your relationships and influence.

You may not see it this way now but giving a presentation always presents an opportunity. It can be a way of promoting yourself or your organisation, getting yourself noticed when it matters or winning new clients.

It's also a way of gaining trust, motivating and encouraging others. So if you think you need a big ego to be a great presenter, forget it! To really win people over any sense of 'me, me, me' has got to go, go, go – which means that you have to genuinely care about the people you are talking to.

This may sound a bit warm and fluffy but it isn't. It is however the key to becoming a great communicator, and ultimately an influential, strong and popular leader – something that I believe has to be earned through effort. (Don't worry at this stage if some of this doesn't make sense – it will by the end of the book.)

First, though, let's start with you as you are now and why you may be the way you are…

The Avoidance Expert

You avoid making presentations like the plague. You do everything and anything possible to escape having to stand in front of an audience and may even seek a career that does not involve making presentations.

Communication skills are at the top of the majority of employers' agendas these days and promotions often depend on you having these skills. Effective communication gets you noticed and brings acknowledgement. It's an area of personal development that can bring great rewards so think of it like you would driving a car. Speaking in front of an audience (like driving a car) is something you can learn to do – and with The Presentation X-Factor you can learn to do it well.

The Reluctant Presenter

You have to do presentations but try and get out of it. Your heart races and you get sweaty palms. You have a fear of speaking in public (and who can blame you!). You may have to do it but do so painfully and with great reluctance, after trying to persuade your apparently more confident colleagues to do the presentation instead of you.

Getting The Presentation X-Factor will help you acquire the necessary skills to give you confidence. With confidence will come enthusiasm and with practice you can come to enjoy making presentations.

Do you avoid making presentations like the plague..?

The Tolerant Presenter

You accept that you will have to give presentations as part of your job but don't seek opportunities to do so. You are probably not very enthusiastic when you make a presentation and may not, for this reason, get a very positive response.

Finding the enthusiasm can turn your presentations into something more successful and therefore more enjoyable. Think of your presentation as a gift to the audience. A presentation is not a test of your knowledge, but a way for you to share it.

The Enthusiastic Presenter

You like doing presentations and look for opportunities to do more. You probably understand that anxiety can be a stimulant which fuels enthusiasm. You almost certainly enjoy presenting because you have experienced some success already, which has given you self-confidence.

By building on your professional communication skills you could become an inspirational speaker. If you are uncertain about why you have success sometimes (but not all the time) then this book will affirm all the things you are doing well and show you how to be certain you reach your audience with your message.

Summary

- Whatever your level of presentation skills, whether you are a beginner or an old hand, you can get The Presentation X-Factor.

- Follow the advice in this book, develop your skills and become a speaker who inspires others.

Fear
is what holds us back –
fear of failure,
fear of what others might think of us.

Break through
the fear barrier
and you will find
your efforts will be
rewarded
many times over.

Chapter 2

Influence, Style And Content

Presenting our ideas in a formal way is not something that comes naturally to the great majority of us. Unlike writing – something we usually learn to do well at school and university – we are rarely taught in earlier life how to present. We're often expected just to get on with it when the time comes.

As a result, many of us simply shy away from the prospect – despite the massive potential for face-to-face communication when it comes to influencing others.

The reasons for this reticence are complex and often to do with our own self-perception. We often don't fully understand the power and psychology of personal presentation and how to speak to an audience's interests.

Think again if you imagine that giving a presentation is just an exercise in giving out information because in reality there is a lot more going on than that – opportunity, influence, persuasion, motivation. Appreciating this can help you take full advantage of the situation.

Raise Your Profile

Making a presentation presents you with an opportunity and as such it is wise to grasp it with both hands because talking to others face-to-face is the best way to make an impression in a very short time.

Think about making the most of the occasion. Be clear about what you would like to achieve. Often there is a need to persuade and/or motivate the audience in what can be challenging circumstances – for example, take presentations about new staff working arrangements, or presenting ideas to the board, or pitching for new work.

Not least, making presentations offers you an opportunity to raise your own profile. This is something to consider seriously – especially if you are looking for promotion. Developing the Presentation X-Factor is going to ensure you stand out from the crowd and that may lead to new work, winning pitches, increased staff productivity, or ultimately your career advancement.

Aiming High
Never be fooled into thinking your presentation is just about giving out information. Information, reports and technical details can all be given out in a document. At the very least you can give a lively and enthusiastic talk that gets you noticed and admired. So even if it is a run-of-the-mill information presentation, you will have to make it interesting to the audience to get them to listen. (See Figure 1: The Hierarchy Of Achievement.)

Your objective is to get the audience to listen. The more they listen the more they hear what you've got to say. And the more they hear what you've got to say, the more they will assimilate it.

This sounds rather obvious, but many of us forget such things in our bid to get the process over and done with as soon as possible.

The Hierarchy of Achievement

The biggest challenge is to MOTIVATE

More often than not you will need to PERSUADE

You can also INFLUENCE

Why just do this? INFORM

To achieve the above you must INTEREST

Figure 1: The Heirarchy Of Achievement

We've all sat through presentations where we realise at the end that we haven't heard or taken on board a single word. If you analyse why, it could be for many reasons – too slow, too boring, too complicated – and none of them will be the fault of the audience.

It's up to you, the speaker, to do what you can to engage your audience – by preparing and delivering a presentation with appeal.

Preparation is a word that makes most of us groan, but there is no getting round the fact that the better you prepare, the more confidence you will have and the more likely you will be able to enjoy the sweet feeling of success at the end of your presentation.

> **TIP!**
> **Recognise how what you say and the way you say it affects those listening to you. You can make people feel discouraged or inspired – it's your choice.**

Again, let me encourage you by letting you know that The Presentation X-Factor formula will help you to prepare in the quickest possible time.

Bringing It All Together

You can broadly separate the art of presentation into two halves – style of DELIVERY and CONTENT. Both must be equally addressed when learning to be an inspirational presenter.

…too long? …too boring? …too complicated?

Getting your style and content right involves understanding the elements that make up a presentation. The successful presenter manages to bring these elements together in a way that has an all round positive impact on the audience. It can help to identify what these elements are before we start to think about preparation for presentations.

CONTENT	DELIVERY
Message	Impact
Angle	Impression
Structure	Appearance
Key points	Voice / Tone
Language	Body language

CONTENT includes the message you offer your audience, the angle you take, structure, key points, the kind of language you use (positive or negative?) and your conclusion.

DELIVERY includes your physical impact, the impression you give, how you look, how your voice sounds, body language and non-verbal communication.

If you think this is starting to look complicated, there is no reason to feel anxious about bringing together the elements of presentation. I will show you how to use The Presentation X-Factor Formula to help you devise your CONTENT – which, let's face it, is the really hard bit.

If you can get that right then it's going to give you the confidence you need to get the DELIVERY right too.

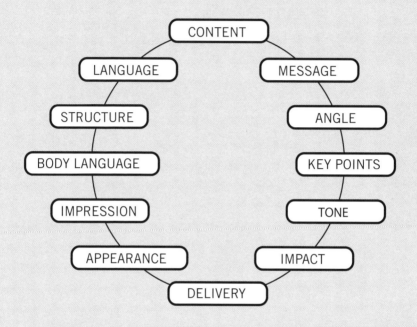

If you can bring all the elements together with integrity, you can be confident of success.

Summary

- Face-to-face communication requires you to find a balance between style of DELIVERY and CONTENT.

- A presentation is an opportunity to inform, influence, persuade and motivate whilst enhancing your reputation.

Chapter 3

How To Be Psychologically Prepared

You've heard it a thousand times before – preparation is the key. And it is!

Take a lesson from the famous American writer Mark Twain who said, "It takes three weeks to prepare a good off the cuff speech."

This time scale may be a slight exaggeration for the majority of presentations, but Mark Twain understood the impact you can have in a very short time and made sure that he was properly prepared to make the most of his opportunity.

And one of the most important aspects of being prepared is to get your psychology right. Or in other words, think about yourself and start to get yourself 'in the zone.'

Think About Yourself

Making presentations requires that you become more self-aware. You have to understand how others perceive you, so that you can use that knowledge to develop skills in building rapport with them.

The first step to pleasing your audience is in how you prepare.

Ask yourself what your reputation is worth – because for every hour you invest in preparation you will reap the benefits in terms of self-confidence and how you come across to others.

Preparing well for a presentation, meeting or any occasion when you want to get a message across, will guarantee that all goes as well as possible 'on the day'. You will feel more comfortable and may even enjoy it!

I'm always meeting people in my training work who hate the idea of 'wasting time' preparing. It's usually because they don't know where to start with it. Sometimes, they claim that they can get by just by standing up and talking 'off the cuff'.

Just occasionally this can work – it's certainly going to be spontaneous and that can be a plus – but it's hard to gain real satisfaction from this way of going about it. You will be none the wiser at the end about why it worked (or didn't, as the case may be).

For most people who try to 'wing it' the result feels like an unmitigated disaster, so do yourself a favour because after all, this is your reputation we are trying to build here. Follow Mark Twain's advice and get prepared. I'll take you through this in more detail later in the book by showing you how to think about what you're going to say, how to condense it, use prompt cards, prepare handouts and of course rehearse – at least twice!

Self-directed Leadership
Making presentations and communicating in an influential way requires that you adopt qualities of leadership – whoever you are and whatever position you have in an organisation.

If you have been asked to give a presentation, it will usually be because you have an area of expertise that others want to know something about. Never see an invitation to present as a test – actually it's an opportunity for you to make your presence felt, to share your ideas and have a positive influence. For many this concept is a challenge and self-belief or understanding that you have something valuable to offer is all-important.

Most of us are resistant to this idea at first. However, making a presentation inevitably influences people, either in a negative, neutral or positive way. You may as well choose to make that influence as positive as you can – and with influence comes responsibility.

Take that responsibility seriously and aim to give your audience something worthwhile. Set out to inspire them by addressing their needs and interests. Aim to make them feel good or empower them.

Accept the opportunity to do more than just give information. Grasp the chance to persuade and motivate people. This takes you into the realm of high-level communication skills. It entails excellent communication coupled with vision – a combination that turns managers into leaders. It is this that is going to give you real impact and the much desired Presentation X-Factor.

Think About The Audience
The way you, the presenter, are feeling about yourself on the day is important. But – and this is where your approach to making presentations may be about to change – the audience are even more important than you, and you have to make them feel important.

*Visualise your audience before you prepare –
cardboard cut-outs optional!*

If preparation is the key to success, it is also true that you can't prepare productively until you have a clear picture of who exactly you will be talking to. It's amazing how many presentations I've seen fail because the speaker hasn't thought about the audience.

Start from a position of respect for them. Before you even begin thinking about what to say, analyse your audience. Build a profile for them. Who are they? What are they interested in? What values do they hold? What concerns or issues do they have? How well informed are they? How do you think they will receive your ideas? What questions will they want to ask?

Take a large piece of paper and jot down the information you come up with, perhaps using mind map bubbles. This will help you to work out the content for your presentation later.

The Audience Attention Span

All audiences have certain things in common. They are self-interested and have short attention spans. You know this because you've sat in audiences yourself – and no, if you thought it was just you, it isn't. So you need to gain and keep your audience's attention by appealing to their interests.

The graph of an Audience Attention Span over the page (Figure 2) represents a mean for most successful presentations, and it really tells us a lot about audiences.

This first graph, of two, shows how audience attention will be at its peak in the first minute. This is the period at the start of the presentation when the audience is weighing up, in a sub-conscious way, whether they like you and are likely to find you interesting, or if they might gain something that will be helpful.

After this peak at the beginning, the audience's attention will subside. This is normal. We all relax a bit once we have the measure of the speaker and what they have to say.

If the speaker has grabbed the audience's interest then they will usually have three peaks of renewed attention before the end when, of course, there will be a huge surge of attention for the concluding thoughts (audiences have a sixth sense about this, and will often spot the end coming even if the speaker doesn't flag it very clearly - although you should).

The second graph (Figure 3) shows you what can happen if you don't successfully grab the audience at the start. Their attention plummets and they don't listen to you. And if people don't listen to you they don't hear your message and your influence is zero – or worse!

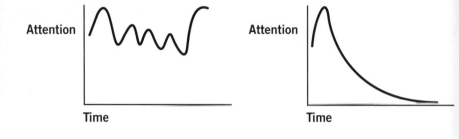

Figure 2	Figure 3

Figure 2 represents the audience attention span for a normal and successful presentation. Figure 3 shows what can happen when you don't grab the audience at the very beginning. It's hard to recover.

Audience attention span is a real challenge that can be overcome when you have thoroughly analysed who you'll be talking to. When you gear your talk towards them it will ensure engagement with them.

Preparing For Each New Audience

It will be clear from the above that there is no getting away from preparing for each different audience. This may mean more work in the short term but it's worth it to give you the confidence you need on the day.

What you will find, however, is that if you often have to speak on the same subject the main body of your talk needs to vary very little. It is mainly the introduction that you really need to work on to make sure your talk is tailored appropriately to the specific audience. You will soon get in the swing of applying The Presentation X-Factor formula – we're coming to it soon – to ensure success on each new presenting occasion.

Experienced presenters learn to ensure that AUDIENCE attention is at a peak when they introduce points they want the audience to fully listen to.

This can be done through emphasis, change of voice or trigger words.

A simple device would be to say, "Now, this is a very important point…"

Psychological Advantage

When you understand that the presentation you give should be a 'gift' for the audience and not in any way about trying to impress them, you will find a subtle difference in how you feel about standing in front of them – and there's likely to be a more than subtle change in the way they regard you. If you prepare with the audience's interests in mind, they will almost certainly be impressed with you anyway.

All too often the opposite is the case. For example, I meet a lot of people who go out to clients with a standard company presentation that takes no account of who they are talking to. Inevitably they will have a miserable experience. The audience may be polite, but they will certainly not be inspired – and the presenter will not gain any satisfaction from their own performance.

> **TIP!**
> If you want to win hearts and minds, clients, contracts, recognition, friends, or influence through face-to-face presentation, then you must put the audience first.

Develop Your Presentation With The Audience In Mind

Having profiled your audience, now you can start the process of shaping the content of your presentation to them.

You will find that this is much easier than if you had no audience in mind at all.

Now ask yourself these questions:

- Why am I doing this?

- What is my objective?

- What is my main message?

- What is it that I want to achieve with the presentation?

- What do I want the audience to go away and do?

- How do I want to change them?

Jot down the answers on your audience profile sheet, and brainstorm about what you might include. Write down or mind map each topic until you can't think of anything else.

It can be helpful to put the paper away for a while and come back to it later. Seeing it with fresh eyes can help you identify quickly what you need to include - or exclude. More than likely the key areas you need to cover will emerge.

Now follow the structuring process that comes next.

Summary

- Preparation is the key to confidence – it's time invested in your confidence and reputation.

- If you're confident, then the audience will have confidence in you.

- Audiences have a short attention span – so pull out all the stops to make your presentation as interesting and relevant to them as possible.

- Making a presentation is not a test of your knowledge but a test of how well you can relate your knowledge and message to your audience.

- Be clear what you want to achieve with the presentation.

Chapter 4

How To Organise Your Content

Think of the presentation in three parts:

- **The Introduction**

- **Main Body Of Talk**

- **Conclusion**

+ **Audio-visual aids – (usually PowerPoint)**

When you are reasonably clear about the general content you want to include, you need to work out your introduction – which, as we've already established, is the most important part of your presentation. It's where you have to grab the audience's attention.

While the introduction for any presentation is the most crucial part of the whole event, in my experience the majority of talks and business presentations completely neglect it.

People often say that it takes audiences less than thirty seconds to make up their minds about you. And it's true.

However advanced your skills are, re-visit the way you open your presentations – because it is usually the make-or-break element.

Some people react badly to the sheer terror of starting a presentation.

The Introduction

The introduction is crucially important, but often the most difficult part of a presentation.

Instinctively, we all know you have to grab the audience from the beginning. Yet many of us don't really stop to think about how we'll open a presentation. Sometimes this may be because the idea of getting started fills us with sheer terror.

If we think about it at all, we often tend to over-elaborate. Grabbing the audience doesn't mean you have to do something clever, or corny, or funny.

We saw from the Audience Attention Span graphs that all eyes and ears are on you at the start. Because of this, that moment when you first stand in front of the audience is psychologically the hardest point in a presentation.

I've seen many presenters take a step back in the first few seconds almost as if they are pushed back by the weight of all that attention on them. The challenge is that this is the very moment when you need to be most in control, most assertive in your body language, and most engaging with your message.

From Rabbit In The Headlights To Leader Of People
Imagine this is a psychological representation of how you feel when you start a presentation:

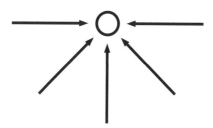

The circle represents you, and the arrows represent the pressures on you. The pressures can be many and take different forms – all of which will combine to stress you out. There might be time constraints on being able to prepare or rehearse, expectations to perform well by your boss or colleagues, risks to your reputation. You may have had a bad journey travelling to the presentation venue and when you finally arrive, you feel horrified to find many pairs of eyes all focused on you.

All this is made far worse if you are not clear about your message and what you want to achieve, and if you are feeling that the whole exercise is some kind of test of your competence. This is often a result of not believing in your own expertise enough to recognise that you really do have something interesting to offer people – if only you can find the right way of saying it.

The pressures can be many and the way you approach them psychologically can really affect the way you feel, the way you come across – and, ultimately, the level of success you gain.

From now on, to avoid the 'rabbit in the headlights' syndrome, I want you to take on this model and think about it when you start every presentation:

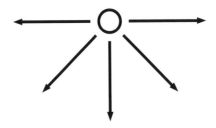

Again the circle represents you. But in this model you resist the pressures through exerting confidence – even if you don't altogether feel it. The arrows represent you filling the space you have been given, sharing information, exerting energy and taking responsibility for the success of the talk.

This means you will have prepared a clear message for the particular audience you are facing. You'll show enthusiasm and warmth with your body language. You'll be focused on making a presentation that the audience can find interesting, relevant and even enjoyable.

Using this model will help you demonstrate many of the attributes of leadership in your presentation. This is something I will expand on later in the book.

I will also offer you some easy-to-follow advice on changing yourself physically, so that through your body language you'll look confident and in control – even if you don't feel it one hundred percent to begin with.

Before you reach that point, though, it is important to get the content of your introduction right.

The successful presentation is one where others have listened eagerly. The way to get them to do that is to make sure the content appeals to them. Your introduction always needs to grab the audience's attention and give them a good reason to listen to you.

Three Easy Steps To A Powerful Start

Step 1: tell the audience what your main message is.

This sounds pretty straightforward but in my experience, a vast majority of business presentations do not do this. In many of them the main message emerges about three quarters of the way through – if you are still alert enough ot catch it. By that time, most people have probably lost interest.

Take time to work out what your main message is and then shape it for the audience you have already analysed and profiled.

Sometimes the best starter is the simplest and most direct.
For example, "I'm here today to show you what my department can do for you."

TIP!
To work out what your main message is start with the words, "I'm here today to show you…" You will often find the answer falls into place. You don't actually need to use these words when you deliver the presentation.
The word 'show' is used deliberately because in your presentation it is good practice not just to explain things, but to illustrate them with examples and stories to make them understand-able and bring colour to your talk.

Other straightforward starters are:

"I'm here today to show you how our company would fulfil the brief you've outlined should we be awarded this contract…"

or "– to show you what you can do to become an excellent presenter…"

or "– to demonstrate how we can become the best sales team next year…"

or "– to offer my recommendations to improve our system for doing…"

Step 2: put yourself into the shoes of the audience and then ask yourself, with complete honesty, this harsh question:
"Why should they listen"?

The truth is that most of us have better things to do if your talk isn't going to be of any interest to us. So you have to give the audience a really good reason to listen. You must grab their attention by appealing to the concerns and issues you identified about them in your preparation.

So this is where your attention grabber comes in. Think of this as a big bold statement. It doesn't have to be backed up in any way at this stage, but it must be relevant to the audience.

Big positive statements that say what you can do for them are always a winner. For example, "My recommendations will ensure that you save money and time and gain even better results than you've experienced in the past…"

Other options for grabbing the audience:

The Shocker
A strongly or starkly worded statistic or statement.
"Last year, enough people died on our roads to fill every seat in Wembley stadium. That is why we are campaigning for more road safety education in schools."

An Anecdote
A short story used to illustrate a point. This is most powerful when it is personalised. People love listening to stories.
"The other day I was in a meeting with a group of marketing managers and they said to me…"

Rhetorical Questions
This device is sometimes overused, but can be effective – especially when combined with strong eye contact. The following example should wake most people up:
"How would YOU like to make a thousand pounds a day?"

Humour
It's a wonderful thing but if you are not naturally funny, don't force it. Just be warm and friendly – whilst maintaining your authortiy. If you do use humour make sure it is relevant and appropriate and never disrespectful or offensive. Being self-effacing can often come into this category. This can be endearing and work well to gain the audience's empathy – but don't over do it.

Step 3: tell them what they are going to get out of your talk.

Staying with this picture of the audience being self-interested (and you only have to think of yourself sitting in an audience to know that this is true) people will really engage with you from the start if they know what they are going to get out of your presentation.

Remember that in most presentations we are trying to persuade others of our ideas or even motivate them – it's a selling job in many respects. People respond best to being sold something if they know how it will benefit them, so be explicit about the benefits your talk hold for them.

You have to pull out the stops
to get people to listen.
If you don't grab their attention
at the beginning
you'll lose them – and then what is the
point?

If
they
aren't listening
they won't hear your
ideas, and
your influence is zero.

The Main Body Of Your Talk

Your introduction must be designed to grab the audience and get their full attention and in that respect will often be a strong and powerful statement without any explanation. It helps, then, to see the main body of your talk as the EVIDENCE or PROOF of your opening statement.

This is the area where you should be on home turf – or in your comfort zone. The challenge is often deciding what to leave out. As we've already established, you have been invited to give a presentation because of your area of expertise, so it can be a challenge to stand back from your accumulated knowledge on the subject and work out what is going to be useful to the audience.

A good way to get started is to limit the key topics you address to just three. You can cover a lot of information but try to group it under one of three headings. Less than three is fine, but you certainly shouldn't try to address more than three – the human brain doesn't like it. Most people are good at remembering things in threes and do not cope well with lots of information in face-to-face situations.

If each key point is a 'learning' point for the audience, then there is no better way to get people to listen and take the learning points away than by illustrating each one with an example, story, anecdote or case study.

This method also makes life easier for you because while you are telling a story you can be very spontaneous and fully engage with the audience.

Examples, Illustrations, Stories, Anecdotes, Case Studies

People really like stories and anecdotes, and to hear about you as a person. This can bring real colour to your presentation – and, let's face it, many business subjects need a little brightening up!

As social beings we humans can't help but be interested in each other, so if you can illustrate a key point with something you have been involved in, the audience is more likely to remember it. Drawing on your own experiences also helps promote the unspoken message, 'I'm an expert'.

One of the reasons your audience remembers points made in this way is because they find it easier to listen to someone telling a story. You become more spontaneous when you are talking about something that happened to you, or a case study you have been involved in, so this is when you can relax and really engage with the audience.

Recommendations And Solutions

Be proactive in making recommendations and offering solutions to issues, based on your expertise. This is something that many presentations lack. Most audiences appreciate being shown the way forward.

People often tell me that their presentation is 'just an overview' of something. (It could be an overview of the last six months, or it could be where Marketing, Finance, or Operations are at the moment, or some similar subject.)

My heart sinks when I hear that word 'overview' because often it means the presentation is going to be a description of where things are at to date – and that tends to be pretty dull because the major part will consist of background, where we are now, and will only nod towards the future.

Often I've seen well-prepared presentations of this type. The speakers have done a good analysis of the situation, and they've identified issues that need to be addressed.

What they don't do, however, is point the way to the future in a meaningful way by using their expertise to make useful recommendations – and even when positive suggestions are included, the presenter doesn't give them enough air time compared to the rest of their presentation.

Another feature of the overview presentation is that the message will often be that we have 'achieved a lot' but will have to 'work harder' too. You know the sort I mean – we've all sat through one. An audience can find the idea of having to work harder very discouraging, especially when the presenter leaves them in the dark about what they need to do – which is often the case.

A successful presentation is one that motivates and if you want to do that you'll have to go that extra mile. Assuming that you want to positively influence or motivate the audience, you will need to bring more to the table in terms of making recommendations for the future, or offering solutions to problems. And you'll need to frame these in a positive way.

What's more, these recommendations, solutions or approaches need to be at the start of the presentation – not left to the end.

Many people who attend my training events, even those at senior level, say they are reluctant to do this because they don't want to pre-empt their bosses. I remind them that those bosses have their own job to do and will probably be grateful for an employee being more pro-active and offering their own expert advice in situations where it might be needed.

In truth many people are sent to my training events by their managers precisely because they are perceived not to be proactive enough or as less than dynamic. Whatever the reason, recognising that you can change this by following The Presentation X-Factor formula will help change the way you are seen not only as a presenter, but possibly also in your role on a daily basis.

The combination of psychology, self-directed leadership and the advice described here will immediately help you to have more impact in your presentations and in wider situations.

Remember you're not there to impress the audience with your knowledge, but to get a message across. Be ruthless in editing out any material that does not immediately enhance your message or help the audience to understand and accept it.

TIP!
Potential clients are always interested in three things: budget, quality and deliverability. So if you are doing a sales pitch you can often do no better than to use these as your three key points.

The Conclusion

All good things come to an end, but most bad presentations simply peter out. Don't let that happen to you. The conclusion is the part of your presentation that most of your audience will hear last. Indeed, it may be the only part they remember. Make it work for you.

To conclude your presentation, sum up and repeat your main message so that your audience is in no doubt about what it is. The end needs to be decisive and powerful so that you leave the audience with a really positive impression to remember you by.

If you do a Question and Answer session (Chapter 7 talks more about Q and A) then repeat your conclusion at the end just to hammer home your main points.

TIP!
A sure fire way of remembering how to prepare a presentation is with my What? Why? How? Presentation X-Factor formula on the next page.

The X Factor Formula
for preparing your presentation

Introduction   After profiling your audience answer
these questions:

                        What? What is my main message?

                        Why? Why should they listen?

                        How? How will it benefit them?

Main Body   Three **Key Points** that provide EVIDENCE or
PROOF of the above:

                        Key Point 1

                        Key Point 2

                        Key Point 3

                        Illustrate each **Key Point** with an example,
story, anecdote or case study.
Include recommendations/solutions

Conclusion   Make it easy for the audience to remember
your talk.

                        **Sum up decisively and repeat your
main message and key points**

Audio-visual Aids

YOU are your best audio-visual aid. People are interested in other people, and part of the pleasure of sitting through a presentation is getting to know and understand the speaker – and perhaps even to be entertained by them.

There *is* a place for audio-visual aids, of course. If your job is to do everything you can to engage and inspire the audience, then audio-visual aids offer you an extra tool to help you achieve that.

Remember the Audience Attention Graph. People have very short concentration spans, so you'll have to work at stimulating their attention if you really want to get your point across. Changing the audience's focus for a short period with an object, sound, video or slide can help you make your point more clearly, and will re-ignite interest if it's waning.

One of my golden rules is only to use audio-visual aids that are really going to enhance your presentation. Don't use them just for the sake of it, or because you think you have to do something 'creative'.

Be creative by all means but YOU must remain the main focus of the presentation.

PowerPoint

These days PowerPoint is the predominant form for audio-visual aids. Love it or loathe it, the chances are you will use it at least sometimes. However, use with caution! We have a saying at Mentor Consultancy, where I'm a Director – **"PowerPoint is powerful… to the point of taking your power away!"**

PowerPoint is a wonderful programme that has helped many people to make presentations who may never have even tried without it. Unfortunately it does seem to have taken over the business world. The phrase 'death by PowerPoint' has entered the English language – and we all know what it means.

The problem is that the big bright screen behind you has the effect of diverting the audience's attention away from you (and you away from them). If there are words on the screen, the audience is much more likely to read them than listen to the presenter – and no audience can do both at once.

So if it's important text that is worth putting on a slide don't talk over it if you think they are reading it – but you can read it out. Yes, you can (even though many people say you shouldn't) because repeating important messages is always good.

Getting the audience to listen to you and absorb your message should be your overriding objective when making a presentation. Sometimes PowerPoint can turn out to be more of a hindrance than a help, so take care to use it to its best effect.

Only introduce slides that help the audience to 'receive' your message. Pictures are generally useful, as long as they are relevant and illustrate what you're talking about. If you really need text, then I recommend you keep it to a minimum – no more than three lines and five words per line.

If you have detailed information you think the audience should have, then produce it as a document you can hand out at the end of your presentation – people can take it away and study it if they're interested. Never hand this out at the start, as they will end up reading it and not listening to you.

Summary for dealing with slides:

- Keep them clear and simple.

- Use good quality pictures and illustrations.

- Use them to illustrate points that are hard to visualise.

- Only use them in a way that enhances your message and to focus the audience's attention.

- Don't use them to try to impress.

- Don't use them as a guide for yourself – they must help the audience to get your message.

- Keep text to a minimum: try for a maximum of three lines with no more than five words per line.

- Prepare a well-presented document as a handout rather than just a copy of your slides.

- Rehearse beforehand so that the technology does not get in the way of your presentation.

- Maintain eye contact with the audience rather than looking at the screen – a common complaint. (That bright screen is so powerful it draws your attention too!)

Remember:

- YOU should be the main focus of your presentation, not your slides.

TIP!
When preparing PowerPoint slides, make use of the notes page to keep notes and comments as you go along.

Handouts

Face-to-face presentations are generally not good vehicles for information and should never be thought of as such. People prefer a document when it comes to taking in facts and figures. Presentations are good for having influence, sharing your ideas, building rapport with significant people and getting them interested in what you are talking about.

So make sure you create a presentation that inspires your audience and give out a handout at the end with all the factual detail they need. Never try to combine the slides you produce as a handout. The two things serve different purposes and you will tie yourself in knots and end up compromising both.

Summary for dealing with handouts:

- Be sure to lay your document out creatively and with maximum readability.

- Put your name and contact number on it.

- Include an executive summary at the start that outlines any recommendations you might be making to the audience.

- Use plain English!

- Give out your handout at the end of your presentation and never at the start when it will be distracting for the audience – if you want them to hear what you say they must listen to you, so you need them to focus on YOU.

Other Issues

Script Or No Script?

Very few people can make a presentation without some notes for guidance. Those that do have often made the same speech many times and just know how to deliver it so that it sounds fresh for each audience.

You have to work out the best system for you. A good system, especially if you are a beginner, is to type out the whole talk and then reduce it right down to a few notes. One of the advantages of doing this is that you can do a word count on your word processor to see how long it is.

Timing

We all speak at a speed of 3 words per second – or near enough. So reckon on about 150 words a minute, allowing for dramatic pauses and the like.

Doing a word count on your script lets you calculate how long the talk will be – and of course you can check the timing later when you rehearse (preferably out loud).

The professional speaker never goes over time and if you are sensible you will, as a matter of course, design your presentation to be slightly shorter than the time allotted.

It's not quantity but quality that counts and most people in your audience won't mind having more time for questions or tea!

Most of the presentations I see in business are twice as long as they need be, simply because they are not focused enough. So focus. Use The Presentation X-Factor formula. Make notes. Rehearse.

Notes

Eventually you should aim to reduce your script to a few notes on note cards or to 'trigger' words or visuals on slides. Ideally you wouldn't need more than five – one each for the introduction, three key points and conclusion. Wait till the run-through stage before doing this though.

Time to throw away the safety net

If you are worried about not having a full script, you are not alone. But now is the time to throw away the safety net and develop the skill of delivering without one. And this will be one of the biggest steps you will take in terms of personal development – ever!

A script can only hold you back in the end, because it is too tempting just to read it – and a script read from the page lacks all the impact, enthusiasm and colour that a well-delivered presentation will have. You will end up feeling depressed about it because you will be trapped by the words on the page and unable to engage with the audience.

The audience will be bored because even if your content is interesting it is almost impossible for most people to concentrate on listening to a script being read.

For one thing the audience needs your eye contact and later on in the book I will take you through some pointers on rehearsal and delivery that you can use to ensure that this does not happen to you.

In the meantime, be certain of three things – that you know what your message is, how you're going to structure the presentation and how you are going to make it appeal to your audience.

TIP!
If you use note cards to keep you on track when delivering your presentation use just five – one for the introduction, one for each key point, and one for the conclusion.

Try to use either notes on paper, or notes on screen. Using both together can mean you end up getting muddled.

Summary

- The first thirty seconds are crucial when it comes to making a positive impression and grabbing your audience's attention.

- Use my What? Why? How? Presentation X-Factor formula to prepare your presentation.

- Develop the Introduction so that the audience is clear about what it is about, why they should be interested and how it's going to benefit them.

- Have no more than three key points in the main body of the talk. Illustrate these with examples, stories and case studies.

- Show leadership by including recommendations and solutions.

- Conclude decisively and repeat your main message.

- If you must use PowerPoint slides then make sure they really enhance your talk. Use pictures and minimum text.

- Additional technical or complicated information can be given out as a handout at the end of the session – never at the beginning.

- If you start out with a full script, extrapolate notes from it and leave it behind.

- Get the timing right – 150 words a minute is a good rule of thumb.

Chapter 5

Before You Go On

You've done all your preparation and you are getting close to the time when you have to make your presentation. It is time to think about how you will deliver it.

Greeting

It's important to devise a warm initial greeting, because the way you welcome everyone and introduce yourself will set the tone of the event.

It seems such an obvious thing to do but in my experience many people find it very difficult to introduce themselves. Bashfulness may have something to do with it – but you will know by now that it is essential to exude confidence right from the moment you take 'the floor'. So decide on the first words you will say when you open your mouth and include these in your rehearsal.

Having a standard introduction is a useful thing to cultivate so that you can articulate the words however stressful the situation. My standard greeting goes something like: "Good morning, everyone. I'm delighted to meet you all and to be working with you today. I'm Tina Coulsting Carter and I'm from Mentor Consultancy where we help people communicate with impact."

Rehearse – For Your Reputation's Sake

Time spent now on rehearsal is an investment in your reputation and your future!

I meet a lot of people who are 'allergic' to rehearsing, but you're mad if you don't at least rehearse your opener – because that's your one opportunity to grab the attention of your audience. You may never get that opportunity again.

Rehearsing your talk is essential. It might seem like a time-consuming effort but it really is the smart thing to do and you'll reap the rewards when you deliver the real thing. Rehearsing allows you to be fully confident of your CONTENT so that you can concentrate on making an impact in the way you DELIVER it.

When you rehearse, do it as if it were the real thing. Say it out loud, and use any technology required. Run through your presentation at least twice, and more often if it is really important. It's your reputation that's at stake here so what is that reputation worth? I'm sure it has got to be worth the time it takes to run through your presentation a couple of times.

If you want honest criticism, ask a member of your family to sit in on the rehearsal. If you want a more positive critique then ask a friend or colleague to listen to a run-through (family can be a bit too blunt sometimes).

There is also the tried and tested 'in front of the mirror' method or, in this age of freely available digital technology, why not video yourself? With video you can make an instant assessment on your level of impact and decide what you need to develop and improve.

It's a good idea to be able to make your presentation with or without PowerPoint.

Control The Environment

Arrange to arrive at the venue early and get a feel for the arrangements. Whenever you can, arrange seating, lighting and visual aids to maximise your impact. YOU should be centre stage so make sure you're not displaced by the projector screen.

If your presentation is to take place during a meeting, arrange to sit with your back to the window. Having the light behind you will give you a psychological advantage, which can be useful if you want to give yourself more authority in the situation.

Check Audio-visual Equipment

We've all been in that nightmare situation where the lights don't dim, the projector's gone missing, the laptop's gone berserk and the marker pens have dried up.

Check all your audio-visual equipment beforehand because these types of mishaps can feel like a real crisis at the time. They may destroy your confidence and make the wrong sort of impact on the audience.

Be sure everything is working. To make things absolutely foolproof it is a good idea to be able to make your presentation with or without PowerPoint. That way, if the dog really does eat your flashdrive the morning of the event then you will be able to cope without it.

Check Out Your Anxiety Levels

Nerves can be a killer, but remember – being nervous is completely normal. A few butterflies in the stomach creates nervous energy which can be channelled into an energetic performance.

You should worry if you feel no nerves at all – have another run-through and ask yourself if it is really going to work for the audience. Try to work up some energy. This is no time for complacency.

If you feel very nervous – feeling sick nervous, or potential 'rabbit in the headlights' nervous, then that could be a problem. If this is you, then you must be meticulous about observing the following rules:

- Organise well, and rehearse. This brings confidence and helps overcome nerves.

- Visualise yourself talking to your audience in a confident and measured way.

- See yourself receiving positive non-verbal feedback from the audience.

- See yourself getting applause at the end of the presentation or people coming up to you enthusiastically.

- See yourself as authoritative and friendly.

- Stick to positive images of a successful presentation.

Exercises To Control Adrenaline

Adrenaline is the substance that travels around your body on the haemoglobin in your blood and is responsible for butterflies in the stomach and a pounding heart. It is the 'fight or flight' drug produced by the body to help in the event of physical emergency – but in the 'captive' situation of a presentation, it makes you feel awful.

There are exercises you can do to control your adrenaline. A drama, yoga or martial arts teacher could show you truly effective exercises to use if you have a real problem with nerves, and working with them will be a well worthwhile investment.

In the meantime, here is a sequence of simple isometric exercises which can help:

- Breathe deeply, from the diaphragm. Imagine that you are sucking up air from the ground into your stomach. You can tell when you're getting this right, because your belly will expand rather than your chest. This will relax you and help you keep control of your voice.

- Tighten the muscles in your toes. Hold for five seconds. Now relax. Repeat this with your calves, thighs and the rest of your body if necessary. Have a good stretch. Feel your body become alert but relaxed.

- Move around. Don't let your body tense up, keep those limbs loose (but don't pace up and down, especially once you're under way!)

Self-esteem

Self-esteem, or the worth we feel for ourselves, can change from day to day and be affected by different situations. Being asked to give a presentation is something that can make many people's self-esteem plummet, because most of us are not trained to make presentations and understandably feel uncertain of our skills.

When we are nervous or anxious we can experience unpleasant physical symptoms such as sweating, shaking, tense muscles, churning of the stomach, headaches. These symptoms make us feel even worse about ourselves so they are something we need to try and combat.

A short-term remedy would be to try and release stress and tension so that you can take control again. There are all kinds of ways of doing this, from the isometric exercises above to reflexology.

Do some research into what might suit you. For a long term change, find ways to be more positive about yourself.

Being More Positive About Ourselves

Self-esteem is the vital ingredient for success and happiness in our lives. When we feel good about ourselves we feel calm, confident and in control.

Don't try to be someone you are not. Making a presentation is a 'performance' but it is not acting.

Just be yourself – but be your very best self. This is what the audience wants.

Be Positive About Yourself:

- Tell yourself lots of encouraging things, like a best friend would. "You're doing really well", "You look great", "You have so many good qualities".

- Say positive things about yourself at all times. Instead of saying: "I can't", say "I'll do the best I can"; "I'm no good at", say "I'm getting better at"; "I always make a mess of things", say "I always learn from my mistakes".

- Avoid being self-critical. Compose positive affirmations for yourself and say them to yourself often. "I am intelligent"; "I am a valuable member of this group"; "I am a good speaker".

- Say to yourself often, "I like and respect myself just the way I am".

All our negative thoughts about ourselves are learnt from things that have been said or done to us in the past.

We can't change what's happened in the past but we can shape the way we want to be in the future by training ourselves to believe positive things instead.

> **"No-one can make you feel inferior without your permission."**
> **Eleanor Roosevelt**

Summary

- Devise a warm greeting and self introduction that you feel comfortable enough to use at any time.

- Always rehearse your presentation in full and out loud. If you are very experienced you should still rehearse the beginning to ensure a smooth and powerful start.

- Take control of the presentation environment. Ensure the arrangements are as you would like them and that the audiovisual equipment is all working properly.

- Work on boosting your own self-esteem and confidence – before you go on, and in your daily life.

Chapter 6

Giving Your Presentation

Here are two words to ponder: AUTHORITY and WARMTH.

These are what all audiences look for in their ideal speaker, albeit sub-consciously. Authority and warmth are essential qualities. If you show them, you'll be guaranteed attention from those you are talking to.

This is fairly easily explained by focusing on audience psychology again.

You have been asked to give a presentation because of your expertise – whether a formal presentation or a more informal meeting to put forward ideas or a report. Whatever the situation, the audience will be looking for something from you – useful information, ideas, recommendations, creativity or leadership.

You may have what the audience wants but if you lack confidence, the audience will lack confidence in you and what you say. Show confidence, on the other hand, and the audience will have confidence in you and what you say.

An audience wants and likes to see someone who carries some authority. At the same time, however, they like to feel that you are on the same wavelength as them. This should be no problem as long as you have done your audience analysis and profiling as discussed earlier. You can use your knowledge about them to 'press the right buttons'.

You can do that in a fairly mechanical way but it really does help to build rapport with people, which means genuinely caring about them and their interests as well as the results of your talk.

The more genuine warmth you put out, the more you will receive back and sometimes this can help you take the edge when it really matters.

Take the situation of a competitive pitch to a potential client for example. You and your opponents will all have similar qualifications and credentials – otherwise you would not have been called. Very often in these situations the decision-making can come down to who the client thinks will not only do the work well, but will also get along with them in a day to day working relationship.

So, while authority and warmth appear to be almost opposing characteristics they really don't have to be. The challenge for you is to be prepared, and rehearse enough to be able to relax and pay some attention to the way you deliver your presentation.

Talk to the audience as individual human beings and see how you gain their respect.

Impression Management

It is important to observe ways to develop your style and body language to improve the impact and authority you have.

The main thing is that you deliver your presentation with passion and communicate enthusiastically. You can't expect to enthuse others unless you yourself are enthusiastic.

You need to manage the impression you give from the start in order to gain the audience's confidence. Remember that the beginning is the hardest part and you need to counter the psychological effect of that stressful situation by making sure that you know your opening sentences inside out.

The start needs all the impact you can muster. We often imagine we are having more impact on a physical level than we really are. It is not until you see yourself on video, for example, that you can see how much more energy you could put into your performance.

While most of us know how we would like to come across, for one reason or another we can't quite put it into practice – usually because of nerves. Nerves can be seriously debilitating and often arise from trying to do something extremely difficult for which you may have had no training. Even very experienced speakers get the shakes because they are often not certain if they've got the presentation right or not.

Whether you are experienced or not, the advice I offer you in this book will help eradicate or at least minimise nerves. The Presentation X-Factor formula and other advice you will find here will ensure that your content targets your audience exactly, enabling you to deliver with the kind of impact that makes your audience sit up and take notice.

Body Language

Body language is also called non-verbal communication for the very reason that it really does communicate so much about you.

Body language is often unconscious but can reveal your innermost self to others. It can convey your opinions, your feelings, your self-image, even your view of the world – even before you start to speak. And it can create a lasting impression. You need to ensure that this lasting impression is a good impression.

	Your 100% IMPRESSION **can be broken down into:**
55%	**Silent speech** **Non-verbal communication**
38%	**Vocalisation** **How you sound, but not what you say**
7%	**The content of your speech**
	From *Silent Messages* **by Professor Albert Mehrabian**

This is all a bit frightening when you come to think about it. The great thing is that you can take control of the impression you give simply by observing and adjusting your body language and psychological approach.

If you can positively change your gestures, you will create in yourself the appropriate mood. So if you make confident gestures you will feel more confident. And if you can make yourself appear more confident, then others will have confidence in you and therefore be more likely to listen to you carefully.

Try it – it really does work.

There are three key pieces of body language that will help you have impact and ensure that you look authoritative, friendly and enthusiastic – even when you don't one hundred percent feel that way. They involve feet, eyes and hands.

Feet: ground yourself
Plant your feet firmly on the floor in line with your shoulders and leave them there. This will give your body a strong and secure foundation that doesn't stop you moving the upper part of your body or using your hands energetically and it will give you instant gravitas and impact. This stance will help you command attention.

It is particularly important to take this position from the first instant. Watch the speaker the next time you are in a presentation. If they haven't had this training then they will invariable take a step back as soon as they open their mouth.

Body language speaks volumes about us and most people read it fairly well (even if subconsciously) and that kind of action undermines the authority and confidence you need to emanate at this stage. Likewise, wobbling about during your delivery is going to say, "I'm wobbly inside". Stand firm - at least for your introduction.

Eyes: make and maintain good eye contact
Look at every member of your audience especially those on the periphery and those who may be showing a lack of interest or even hostility.

If it is a large audience then mentally break it up into sections and give each section your eye contact in turn.

If making eye contact is difficult for you it is a skill worth learning, because it will make a lot of difference to the feedback you get from others. You could start by looking at peoples' foreheads – they probably wont be able to tell the difference but do make an effort to get this right. It will pay off for you.

Keep the eye contact at a comfortable level for people so that it doesn't turn into a stare.

Hands: use natural open gestures
Using your hands naturally with open gestures is absolutely crucial for generating energy into the room. Open gestures generally means that your arms are open and away from your body and the palms of your hands are facing up most of the time.

Face your audience and control your gestures positively. In other words, take care of absent minded gestures like fiddling or playing with your hair. In my consultancy work I've seen all sorts of involuntary body language over the years – one man actually pulled up his sweater and started scratching his stomach and never realised he was doing it!

If you have been told to put your hands behind your back and not wave them about – as a lot of my trainees say they have – then it's just plain wrong. If you want proof of this, body language experts Alan and Barbara Pease, authors of *The Definitive Book of Body Language*, can provide it. Their extensive research found that audiences respond 84% more positively and listen more to speakers who use their hands in a positive way. Interestingly this reduced to 52% when speakers used palm-down gestures and to only 28% when they used pointing gestures.

TIP!
Important body language for a confident and friendly appearance:

- **Keep feet firmly on the ground, standing still and straight**

- **Keep good eye contact with everyone in the audience**

- **Use your hands expressively and make open gestures**

Take care with your appearance – and smile
Along with body language, your very appearance is a form of non-verbal communication. Image and grooming can effect that all-important first impression especially if you have not taken enough care over it.

Go for an outfit 'one notch up' from the one you first thought of, if it is an important presentation. Aim for smart, comfortable, and attractive. And if this is something you've not given much time to thinking about maybe this is the time to go out and buy that new suit.

How is your hair/beard? Is it clean and tidy? If you wear make-up – is it well applied and subtle? How do you carry your head? Women especially – watch out for that little girlie 'head on one side' thing. Tilted too far back? Try lowering your chin – this will help to lower your voice too. Nervousness tends to make our voices go up in pitch.

Remember to smile. Making a presentation is a serious business but aim to put your self across as a friendly person as well as an authoritative one.

Two-way non-verbal communication
So far we've focussed on positive body language. But other (more negative) body language can give away quite a lot about how we are feeling as a presenter:

- Touching the hair or face shows nervousness.

- Touching the nose shows you may not be telling the truth or, more likely, 'making it up as you go along'.

- Holding something in front of you shows you are trying to protect yourself from the audience.

- Holding your hands behind your back means you will be holding your energy back.

- Arms folded means you are defensive.

- Feet facing away from the audience shows you want to get away.

- Peering over glasses or putting glasses on and off can make you look less than professional – it may be time to invest in a pair of Varifocals!

These are just a few examples, and again Alan and Barbara Pease's books will give you a lot more information on this subject.

The more you learn, the more effective you'll be, because just as you the presenter can give away feelings through body language so can your audience or colleagues in meetings. If you can learn to read the body language others transmit then it can help you to know how to handle them and what to say.

Look out for these gestures from others in critical situations:

- If people start fingering or hiding their mouths, they have difficulty believing what you say. If they do so while answering questions they in turn are being deceitful.

- Stroking the chin is an evaluation gesture or make-your-mind-up time. Another is a hand to the side of the face. Beware the chin support, this can mean boredom.

- Crossed arms reflect negative or defensive thoughts. Such is the strength of this gesture that it will work in reverse. Give people reason to shift position – by asking a question, for example.

- Taking their spectacles off indicates that the person has had enough. Maybe your subject matter is getting too complicated or your presentation has been going on too long. This is a very useful piece of body language to take note of, especially in a pitch or sales situation.

Avoid Over-use Of Notes

Make the words flow from your mind, not off the page. Use only key words on cards or slides as memory aids. Key words should act as triggers for the next part of the presentation.

PowerPoint slides can act as memory aids – but never produce slides just for your own benefit. This can lead to boring slides full of text and to you looking at the screen more than the audience – thus undermining any real impact you might have.

Rehearsal will help you work from minimal notes but don't go too far and memorise a whole script. Reading off a page sounds monotonous so people don't listen, but repeating something by heart sounds just as bad in a different way – because it loses any spontaneity.

It doesn't matter if you say everything perfectly, it is the essence of the messages you want to get across that is important.

It is much better to take time to rehearse and get familiar with what you want to get over to the audience. This way the audience will feel that you are really connecting with them.

Avoid over-use of notes.

Voice

Everything about your presentation should reach out to the audience and that goes for your voice too. Talk to the audience like you would to a friend – but without losing authority and control.

Use your voice to force the audience's attention when it is needed. For example, vary the pace of your voice. Try slowing it down or speeding it up for effect. Vary the tone and pitch to give light and shade. Think about how storytellers keep children spell bound with their voices.

Low and slow: "There once was a strong and powerful king…"
Light and quick: "…and he had a clever and beautiful daughter…"

This is something that takes practice but when you are fully committed to making the presentation a success from the point of view of the audience, you will find that your voice changes naturally with your whole approach.

For example, if you tend to speak too quickly, it is probably because you want to get the presentation over and done with. However, when you focus on what the audience needs you will want to deliver in a more measured way so that they can follow your words and assimilate your message.

So don't get too hung up on voice at this stage.

Try these tips:

- Before you go on, reduce tension as far as possible with relaxation exercises such as deep breathing. Tension can strangulate the voice.

- Really mouth your words. This will slow you down and give clarity. Try an exercise where you mouth words silently across a room to a partner, to see if they can understand what you are saying.

- Introduce one to two second pauses into your speech at appropriate points to create drama. This can take practice but if you 'script' them in and then rehearse it will help you develop a more engaging voice pattern. Think of Churchill!

- Vary the volume of your voice purposefully. Have you ever noticed how some people will shout about trivial things like the traffic or rain but they will speak very quietly about something that is really important that they want you to listen to.

- Lower your voice. Try lifting your head from your chest and then speak. This can help bring the pitch of your voice down.

- Practice projecting your voice. For fun, recite a bit of Shakespeare and make sure they can hear you in the dress circle. It really does help your voice and gets you in the mood for being heard!

TIP!
Recite Shakespeare **LOUDLY** to give your voice a work out: Imagine leaping out from the wings to deliver this piece, from Henry V, Prologue, Act 1, full force on stage.

O for a muse of fire that would ascend
The brightest heaven of invention,
A kingdom for a stage, princes to act
And monarchs to behold the swelling scene!
Then should the warlike Harry, like himself,
Assume the ports of Mars; and at his heels,
Leash'd in like hounds, should famine, sword and fire
Crouch for employment.

Positive Language

I hope that by now you've got a good idea of how to structure a presentation and how to select content. But if you want to really build up a rapport with the audience or get people on side, you'll need to think about how you say things.

There are obvious rules on language – like being clear and direct, avoiding jargon as much as possible and where you can't, ensure you define it.

In this section I want to focus on the idea of using positive language.

Using positive language will make you a much more appealing person to listen to. Similarly, using negative language can give the audience a negative feeling about you. Try turning all negative statements into positive ones. This is not difficult once you get the hang of it and it is possible to put a positive slant on almost anything you may need to talk about.

Consider these statements:
"Last year we were the worst sales team in the whole of our region and we are going to have to work very hard to change that this year…"

"This year I want you to be the best sales team in our region. And I'm going to show you how we can develop from our current level to reach that goal."

The first statement is going to make an already unmotivated team feel even less motivated. They will feel criticised and bad about themselves. And when you tell them they are going to have to work harder – well then they will really lose interest.

There may be a lot of reasons why a team hasn't performed, but often leadership is a critical factor. So in this situation you have to show leadership to motivate others.

Good leaders encourage and guide others and they are trusted because they have confidence and show that they have confidence in others. Positive language does all these things for you.

If you analyse those statements you'll sense leadership in one, but not the other.

The first statement may sound inclusive by using the word WE but it does not help in a fundamentally negative announcement. The second statement contains some special words that are crucial to use in order to engage others.

Look at the strength of the second statement. This positive statement uses two of the most important words in the English language especially when it comes to presenting ideas to others – YOU and I!

TIP!
Get used to using positive phrases like "I believe" and "I recommend". These can be subtly powerful when persuasion is required.

The Most Powerful Word

When it comes to face-to-face presentation YOU (or YOUR) is the most powerful word you can use. Listen to some business presentations and you wont hear it once. How then do they expect to engage with the audience?

If you use my Presentation X-Factor formula for structuring the presentation it will be difficult to omit the word YOU because the aim of that formula is to make your presentation very audience-focused.

If you have a script, go through it – how many sentences can you change to include the word YOU?

Try it.

Even simple changes such as from "We are equipped to do this that and the other" to, "This is what we can do for YOU" makes all the difference.

If you have done your homework you can match up what you know they want with what you can do for them.

Another example – using the word YOUR this time:

"We can do this for staff" to "We can help YOUR staff…"

Use every opportunity to use the word YOU or YOUR and it will transform the level of rapport you have with your audience.

Another Powerful Word
Using the word 'I' gives you a lot of authority. It means you are taking responsibility for the situation.

Many people don't like to use the 'I' word because they imagine it is only appropriate to talk on behalf of their organisation and therefore never stray from using the word WE.

But see how much stronger this statement will appear to a potential client.

"We will ensure that you get that information immediately."

This sounds positive enough but subconsciously the client will not know who is taking responsibility for getting them what they want, and may suspect that no-one will.

"I will ensure that you get that information immediately."

This leaves the client in no doubt about who is taking responsibility.

There is another reason many people do not like using the 'I' word and that is because they think that you should not get personal in a presentation or that it might be conceived as arrogant. Not true – but it depends on your approach.

If you talk about yourself in terms of how you can help those in front of you, in an explicit way, then they will be clamouring to know more. If on the other hand you just give a string of details about how well qualified you are, with an implicit idea that these will be useful to them, then this could easily be seen as showing off for no good reason.

Consider these two statements that may be used in an interview situation:

"I'm extremely well qualified to do this job. I've worked for Joe Bloggs Ltd, where I won an award for this, that and the other and have 10 years experience in this field."

"I will use my experience and qualifications to ensure I do the best job possible for you. For example, I believe you would like this that and the other to happen. When I worked for Joe Bloggs Ltd I did this, that and the other which brought widespread recognition for that company and I believe I can do the same for you."

The second statement will be much more appealing to the prospective client or employer because they can see immediately how you can be of value to them.

Use the same technique when selling ideas to colleagues or staff:

"We are making changes, and here is what is going to happen".

"I'm here to show you how your roles are going to be affected by changes coming up".

This second statement shows personal responsibility by using the word I plus a caring attitude by using the words YOU and YOURS.

My Presentation X-Factor formula promotes the use of personal examples, stories, anecdotes and case studies to illustrate points and reinforce messages. It will be difficult to do that meaningfully without using the 'I' word.

Use the 'I' word with strength and pride!

Summary

- Audiences like (and therefore listen to) presenters who emit authority and warmth at the same time.

- You need to manage the impression you give others through positive body language, voice and appearance.

- Learn to read your audience's body language and respond accordingly.

- Use positive language.

- Use the most powerful word in communication often – YOU.

- To boost your authority and to gain audience confidence use the word – I.

Chapter 7

Questions And Answers

You've sweated for hours to perfect and hone your presentation and put your all into presenting it with impact, but here's a thing: for many an audience, the most important part is yet to come. It's the Q and A session at the end. No wonder many presenters dread it – because now the audience is in control, or appears to be.

However, a positive view of your own expertise will help your psychology here. Remember that if you've been invited to give a talk it is because you have a field of expertise others are interested in. Sometimes there may be people in the audience who know more than you but this is your 'show', not theirs, so stay in control of the event till the end. Never forget you are there for the audience and they like to see someone who is really in charge.

They won't even mind if there are questions you can't answer as long as you are honest about it.

Follow these rules and you will sail through the Q and A:

• Anticipate awkward questions and think through responses, but don't rehearse them so that they come out too pat.

• If you think the audience may not have heard the question,

REPEAT IT. It is courteous, and it will give you a little more thinking time (we think twice as fast as we can speak).

- Return to your prepared messages and use the bridging techniques below to deal with 'hijackers' and questions that are going to take you away from the points you are trying to make. Don't be led into an area you don't want to go.

- If you do not know the answer to a question, say so – but also try to offer something to the audience: "I don't know the answer to that but what I do know is…" or "I don't know, but I can find out and get back to you…"

- Answer the whole audience, not just the questioner. Begin with a second or two of eye contact to the questioner then move on to include the others.

- To avoid that horrible silence you can get when you ask for questions, you might consider 'planting' someone in the audience with a question to get the ball rolling.

- If there is no independent chairman, YOU decide when the session has gone on long enough and bring it to a close in a controlled way. Don't let it just peter out.

- After questions, do sum up your key points again before ending – remember it is the last thing people hear and take away with them.

Building Bridges

Question and Answer sessions are a great opportunity for people to ask 'daft' and irrelevant questions. Don't let your session get hijacked. Always acknowledge a question politely but don't allow yourself to be taken off on a tangent. This is where the bridging technique comes in handly. Construct a bridge to bring the audience back to your own message.

Some examples of 'bridges':
"Whatever the rights and wrongs of that, I believe..."

"Let's put this in context..."

"That's a fair point, but…"

"I understand that many people do believe that, but..."

"That's not the real issue here. What's more important is..."

"That's a complex question and I'd be happy to discuss it in detail with you later. In the meantime let me say…"

"I can't answer that question (because…), but what I can tell you is…"

We're approaching the end of *Get the Presentation X-Factor!* now and unless you need the next chapter, which explores Presenting In A Group, I suggest you turn straight to Chapter 9 for the Action Plan.

Chapter 8

Presenting In A Group

Increasingly in business, a 'beauty parade' system is used as part of the selection procedure for suppliers. You will usually wish to present your team – and if you do so, it is essential to illustrate by your presentation that you do work as a team.

Working as a group is also worth considering whenever you want to add variety and pace to your presentations – but beware, if you do not follow the advice below, this can become counter-productive and give people the wrong impression entirely. A chain is only as strong as its weakest link.

Have an initial planning meeting involving all presenters. This is essential and should get everyone to focus on who the audience or potential client is and what their needs and interests are before using the magic formula to think about the presentation itself.

This meeting need not last long, but should be used to establish your main messages and key points: who does what, the ground to be covered by each presenter, the time allotted together with the overall structure of the presentation.

Nominate a 'chairman'. They should prepare opening and closing statements. The chairman's most important functions are to settle procedures such as handovers and use of slides, to check the presentation environment (layout, audience numbers, equipment etc), and to make sure everyone else is clear about their role, main message and focus.

Each presenter prepares their own contribution following the Presentation X-Factor formula – keep in mind that when there is more than one presenter, simplicity and brevity are doubly important.

Time must be made for a final full-scale rehearsal, preferably the day before presentation which will allow time for amendments should they be needed.

Remember to include handovers and visual aids. The handovers should be as seamless as possible and one way to get this right is to ensure each presenter knows the final words of the previous presenter.

If you don't think a full rehearsal is necessary then just think about what a successful presentation may be worth to you in terms of reputation and possibly thousands of pounds worth of future work.

Rehearsal will ensure confidence and confidence is the all important ingredient. Support each other on the day by looking interested in what your colleagues are saying. Sitting in a corner looking bored will give an impression of a team in disunity.

Developing your team until it has The Presentation X-Factor will be very empowering for each of its members. It will bring success for you in pitches, presentations and meetings – and of course an empowered team is a happy team.

Chapter 9

Action Plan

Finally you've done all the reading, so now you must go away and put what you've learnt into practice. Practice does make perfect and will give you The Presentation X-Factor in no time.

To help you get there, use the checklist below. Tick off the areas you want to concentrate on developing and improving.

Planning Your Talk

- Check out your audience. Who are they? What are their concerns and issues? What are you trying to achieve with your talk?

- Decide what your main message is and the angle you want to take to suit the audience. Be clear about how it will benefit the audience.

- Where and when is the talk? What facilities do they have there?

- Map out your ideas and link them to your objective. Will they serve to achieve the outcome you want?

- Order and prioritise ideas under no more than three key headings.

- Use the Presentation X-Factor formula as a quick reminder on preparation.

- Say it out loud and write it down. You can extrapolate notes from it later.

- If you must have or need PowerPoint, then design slides for the audience and not as a guide for you. Find some relevant and inspiring pictures.

- Keep it simple and keep to time by rehearsing. 150 words = 1 min.

Structure

- The opening must tell the audience what your main message is and grab their interest. Follow up by telling them how they will benefit from listening to you.

- The main part of the talk includes your key points. Add colour to emphasise and prove important points with examples and personal experiences.

- The conclusion should repeat the main message, summarise important points and end decisively and up beat.

- Use PowerPoint slides only where they enhance your talk or illustrate points.

Language And Style

- Use ordinary conversational language.

- Avoid jargon or if you must use specialist words then make sure you define them.

- Always use positive language.

- Empathise with your audience – show you understand their needs.

- Emphasise important points by changing tone of voice or using trigger words.

Delivery

- Start very still with feet planted on the ground.

- Speak out to the audience with your voice and with your hands. Relax, smile, use open body language – be confident.

- Retain good eye contact with the audience.

- Use your hands to gesticulate and avoid wringing, fiddling and other distracting behaviour!

- A good knowledge of your material will allow you to appear more spontaneous. Avoid reciting, reading a script and/or learning the talk of by heart but do rehearse.

- Vary the pace and tone of the talk.

Qualities To Cultivate

- Empathy (understanding others' needs)

- Confidence

- Clarity

- Integrity

- Leadership

- Enthusiasm

- Warmth

- Capability

Strive Towards Being Someone Who

- Is inspirational

- Listens

- Empowers

- Is well informed

- Sets an example

- Is in control

- Is reassuring

- Makes others feel valued

- Can make recommendations

- Shows others the way

- Addresses conflict openly and fairly

- Understands the bigger picture

A Final Encouraging Note

You've come to the end of this book so you know how to get The Presentation X-Factor!

Now I want you to go out and get it.

Fight the fear that might want to stand in your way and just do it – what's the worst that can happen?

Take it from someone who knows what it's like to be inarticulate with trepidation when even just introducing myself at a meeting – anyone can do this.

By putting into practice the advice you've read here and preparing with my Presentation X-Factor formula you can become excellent at presentations, anytime, anywhere, to anyone.

The overall effect of presenting enthusiastically with energy, genuine empathy for your audience and a desire to empower them in some way will strongly affect others' perception of you. You can and will really inspire audiences and be someone other people like to listen to.

Take every opportunity to present yourself with impact, and your standing as someone with influence and leadership qualities will be enhanced, and I don't believe it is any exaggeration to say that your life will change for the better.

Do all the things you've identified you need to do and you will develop the special kind of impact that defines the Presentation X-Factor.

I wish you the very best for the future.

Success!

Presentation X-Factor Summary

- Carry out a profile of your audience.

- What's your main message? "I'm here today to show you..."

- Think of a 'grabber': an opener that is going to give this particular audience a reason to listen and get their attention.

- Explain how your audience will benefit from your talk.

- Include no more than three key points backed up with examples, illustrations or stories, personalised for colour. Don't forget recommendations and solutions.

- Finish in a decisive way with a striking sentence that summarises your message and makes an impact that will stay with your audience.

- PowerPoint slides should be relevant and enhance your talk. Use pictures more and text less.

- Rehearse out loud.

- Boost your energy, control the adrenaline with breathing exercises or tensing and relaxing muscles and stretching – be positive.

- Deliver with Passion, Integrity, Warmth and Confidence!

- Use positive and reassuring language.

NOTES